easy learning

Comprehension bumper book

Ages 7–9

Helen Cooper

How to use this book

- Easy Learning bumper books help your child improve basic skills, build confidence and develop a love of learning.

- Find a quiet, comfortable place to work, away from distractions.

- Get into a routine of completing one or two bumper book pages with your child every day.

- Ask your child to circle the star that matches how many questions they have completed every two pages:

Some = half or fewer   Most = more than half   All = all the questions

- The progress certificate at the back of this book will help you and your child keep track of how many ⭐ have been circled.

- Encourage your child to work through all of the questions eventually, and praise them for completing the progress certificate.

- Make sure your child has some paper to continue their answers on where necessary.

- Use the 'My words' pages (pages 62–63) to make a note of any words in the texts that your child is not familiar with.

- Encourage them to use a dictionary to look up the meanings.

- Ask your child to find and colour the little bookworms that are hidden throughout this book.

- This will help engage them with the pages of the book and get them interested in the activities.

Parent tip
Look out for tips on how to help your child learn.

ACKNOWLEDGEMENTS

Published by Collins
An imprint of HarperCollinsPublishers Ltd
1 London Bridge Street
London SE1 9GF

© HarperCollinsPublishers Limited 2017

ISBN 9780008212414

First published 2017

10 9 8 7 6 5 4 3 2 1

All images and illustrations are
© Shutterstock.com and
© HarperCollinsPublishers

The author and publisher are grateful to the copyright holders for permission to use the quoted materials:

Page 4 An extract from *The Worst Witch* by Jill Murphy. Published by Puffin Books, Penguin Books Ltd. Copyright © 1974 Jill Murphy.

Page 10 'The Sound Collector' by Roger McGough from *All the Best*. Published by Penguin Books Ltd. Copyright ©Roger McGough.

Page 18 'The Skyfoogle' from *Kaleidoscope: Band 15/Emerald*, pages 11–18 (text only). Published by Pearson Australia. Reproduced with permission from Carthew, M. and Rosen, M.

Page 20 'Write-a-Rap Rap' from *My Hat and All That* by Tony Mitton. Published Random House Children's Publishers UK. Copyright ©Tony Mitton. Reproduced by permission of the author and David Higham Associates Ltd.

Page 24 *London Zoo gorilla broke enclosure twice before escape.* Copyright ©Guardian News and Media Ltd 2016.

Page 30 'Dear Mum' from *Thawing Frogs* by Brian Patten. Published by Puffin, 2003. Copyright ©Brian Patten. Reproduced by permission of the author c/o Rogers, Coleridge and White Ltd.

Page 36 An extract from *Flat Stanley* by Jeff Brown. Published by Egmont UK Limited and used by permission of HarperCollins Publishers. Text copyright © 1964 The Trust u/w/o Richard Brown a/k/a Jeff Brown f/b/o Duncan Brown.

Page 50 An extract from *The Iron Man* by Ted Hughes. Published by Faber and Faber Ltd. Copyright ©Ted Hughes.

All rights reserved. No part of this publication may be reproduced, stored in a retrieval system, or transmitted, in any form or by any means, electronic, mechanical, photocopying, recording or otherwise, without the prior permission of Collins.

British Library Cataloguing in Publication Data.

A CIP record of this book is available from the British Library.

Author: Helen Cooper
Commissioning Editor: Michelle I'Anson
Editor and Project Manager: Rebecca Skinner
Cover Design: Sarah Duxbury
Text Design & Layout: Paul Oates and Q2A Media
Production: Paul Harding
Printed in Great Britain by Martins the Printers

Contents

Modern fiction: The Worst Witch

Maud and Mildred were sharing a cauldron, of course, but unfortunately neither of them had learned that particular spell.

'I think I can remember it vaguely,' whispered Maud. 'Bits of it, anyway.' She began to sort through the ingredients which had been laid out on each workbench.

When everything was stirred together in the cauldron, the bubbling liquid was bright pink. Mildred stared at it doubtfully.

'I'm sure it should be green,' she said. 'In fact I'm sure we should have put in a handful of pondweed-gathered-at-midnight.'

'Are you *sure*?' asked Maud.

'Yes …,' replied Mildred, not very definitely.

'*Absolutely* sure?' Maud asked again. 'You know what happened last time.'

'I'm *quite* sure,' insisted Mildred. 'Anyway, there's a handful of pondweed laid out on each bench. I'm positive we're supposed to put it in.'

'Oh, all right,' said Maud. 'Go on, then. It can't do any harm.'

Mildred grabbed the pondweed and dropped it into the mixture. They took turns at stirring it for a few minutes until it began to turn dark green.

'What a horrid colour,' said Maud.

'Are you ready, girls?' asked Miss Hardbroom, rapping on her desk. 'You should have been ready minutes ago. A laughter potion should be made up quickly for use in an emergency.'

From The Worst Witch *by Jill Murphy*

The Worst Witch is a fantasy story about life in a school for witches. Look at the different types of punctuation used.

1 Answer these questions in full sentences.

Maud and Mildred are just learning to make spells.
What does Maud say at the beginning of the extract that tells you this?

_____

_____

Find **three adverbs or phrases** that show the girls are not confident about their spell-making.

_____

Would you trust Maud and Mildred to make you a potion?
Give a reason for your answer.

_____

_____

2 Find the missing words in the text.

_____ stared at it doubtfully.

'I think I can remember it _____,' whispered Maud.

'I'm quite sure,' _____ Mildred.

Parent tip
Use this text to talk to your child about how to use speech marks correctly.

3 Who said it? Write **Maud** or **Mildred**.

'I'm sure it should be green.' _____

'Bits of it, anyway.' _____

'Go on, then. It can't do any harm.' _____

'I'm positive we're supposed to put it in.' _____

How much did you do?   ## Questions 1–3

Circle a star
to show how much
you have done.

 Some

Most

 All

5

Acro"bats" Adventure Park

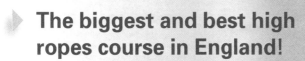

> ## The biggest and best high ropes course in England!

Use your skill and daring!

- fun for all the family
- giant games and balancing challenges
- swing through the trees
- leap from a height
- 70 activities
- from 60 cm to 16 m high

- test your strength, balance and agility
- fly through the air
- hang from the branches
- cross a wobbly world
- three levels of difficulty
- spread over five acres of forest

What are you waiting for?

For our younger adventurers	Feeling more confident?	Brave and bat-like?
• The green course • For children up to 6 years old	• The orange course • Up to 14 years (or up to 160 cm)	• The red course • From 14 years (or over 160 cm)

Your safety is our priority!

- Helmets and safety harnesses provided
- Gloves for gripping and perfecting those bat moves!
- Safety training talk before you start
- Trained guides to help you – look out for the guys in green!

When you need a break, swing down from the trees and enjoy our facilities:

- ○ The Bat Cave, our award-winning cafe, serving delicious home-made organic meals and snacks
- ○ Our picnic area – tables, benches and rubbish recycling provided
- ○ Eco-toilets

CONTACT US:

Acro"bats" Adventure Park
Chippington Wood, Sawley SW5 TEE

Open daily 9am–7pm
5 minutes from J21 of the M98

www.acrobatsadventurepark.co.uk
Facebook: Acrobats adventure park
Twitter: @Acrobats_adventure
Telephone: 04245 712349

Look out for powerful verbs and exclamation marks.

1 Tick (✓) the correct answer.

Which course is most suitable for young children? red ☐ green ☐

Which safety item is provided? a helmet ☐ wings ☐

Where is the adventure park? Sawley ☐ Acro"bats" ☐

How many activities are there? 70 ☐ 60 ☐

Parent tip
Ask your child to collect leaflets that are good examples of persuasive writing.

2 Find words and phrases in the text to answer these questions.

Find and copy **two phrases** that are used to persuade you to use the cafe.

_____

Find **three verbs** that describe how you might move around the adventure park.

_____

Put the courses in order of difficulty, from the hardest to the easiest.

_____

3 Give your answers using full sentences.

Why do you think the name Acro"bats" was chosen for the high ropes course?

_____

_____

Why do you think the leaflet tells you that the adventure park is near to a motorway?

_____

How does the leaflet try to reassure you that the park is very safe? Give **three** examples.

_____

How much did you do? Questions 1–3

Circle a star to show how much you have done.

Some

Most

All

Non-fiction: Contents page

Contents

Written by Ali Carson

Photography by Benji Plane

A contents page is used at the front of a book to tell you what you will find in the book.

1 Use the text to help fill in the missing words.

The subject of this book is _____ .

The book is written by _____ .

The chapter about eco-vehicles starts on page _____ .

The _____ is on page 34.

2 Answer these questions with a sentence.

What do you think would be a good title for this book?

_____

How do you know that this is a non-fiction book?

_____

Where in the book would you find the index?

_____

Where would you look in the book to find out what a word means?

_____

3 Circle the correct page number.

Which page might tell you about aeroplanes?	2	10
Which page might tell you about submarines?	6	14
Which page might tell you about steam trains?	22	26

Parent tip
Make sure your child can use a contents page, index and glossary to find information.

How much did you do?   Questions 1–3

Circle a star
to show how much
you have done.

 Some

 Most

 All

Modern poem: The sound collector

A stranger called this morning
Dressed all in black and grey
Put every sound into a bag
And carried them away

The whistling of the kettle
The turning of the lock
The purring of the kitten
The ticking of the clock

The popping of the toaster
The crunching of the flakes
When you spread the marmalade
The scraping noise it makes

The hissing of the frying pan
The ticking of the grill
The bubbling of the bathtub
As it starts to fill

The drumming of the raindrops
On the windowpane
When you do the washing-up
The gurgle of the drain

The crying of the baby
The squeaking of the chair
The swishing of the curtain
The creaking of the stair

A stranger called this morning
He didn't leave his name
Left us only silence
Life will never be the same

Roger McGough

**Look at how this poem uses rhyme and sound
(onomatopoeia) to create powerful images.**

1 Draw a line to match each sound to an object.

ticking		drain
popping		curtain
drumming		clock
swishing		toaster
gurgle		raindrops

Parent tip
Poetry can be challenging for children. Talk to your child about what they think the poet is saying.

2 List your **four** favourite **sound verbs** from the poem.
Explain why you chose each verb.

_____

_____

_____

_____

3 Describe the mood that the poet creates at the beginning and end of the poem.

_____

_____

_____

4 What do you think would happen if the sound collector came along and removed all the sounds from our world?
Write your answer on a separate piece of paper.

How much did you do?   Questions 1–4

Circle a star
to show how much
you have done.

☆ Some   ★ Most   ★ All

Recount: A day at Mum's work

Last Friday, we had a day off school. There was no one to look after me, so I had to go into work with my mum. I had to wake up very early. It's quite a long walk to the train station. We had to run along the platform to catch our train! Luckily, we managed to get on it in time, but it was very busy, so we had to stand up. It was also very hot and sweaty. Yuck!

After we got off the train, we had to walk for a bit through lots of busy crowds, so I had to hold hands with Mum. It was quite scary! Finally, we arrived at the office where Mum works. I had to sign in at the reception desk at the front of the building. The man behind the desk was very nice and he gave me some sweets, but Mum said I couldn't have them until after lunch.

Mum is an architect. She has designed some weird buildings, which is cool, but she also does more boring stuff, like our next-door neighbour's kitchen. She had lots of jobs to do on her computer and she said that I had to sit next to her and be patient whilst she did them. Although I had my books with me and other activities to do, it was much more fun to swirl around on the swivel chair that I was sat on! It made me feel queasy after a while though, because I was so dizzy. A lady sat near to us gave me a very cross look when I nearly fell off!

When it was time for lunch, Mum took me to a nearby café. I ordered a hot chocolate to drink, which was delicious but burned my tongue when I first took a sip from it. Mum was feeling extra generous, so she even let me have a brownie as well. (She must have forgotten about my sweets.) How lucky!

When we got back to the office, Mum had to go to a meeting that I wasn't allowed to go to, so I hung out at her desk and chatted to the man who sits across from her. At 5 o'clock it was time to go home. I'm glad I don't have to do that every day!

A recount retells a sequence of events in the order that they happened.

1 Use words from the box to finish each sentence.

swivel chair	Friday	hot chocolate	train	architect

School was closed on _____.

Mum is an _____.

The author enjoyed drinking _____.

They travelled to work by _____.

The _____ spun round.

Parent tip
Ask your child to tell you about a day out. See whether they sequence events correctly.

2 Answer each of these questions with a sentence.

Why was the train 'very hot and sweaty'?

_____

_____

Do you think the narrator enjoyed going to work with their mum? Explain why.

_____

_____

What might the lady in the office have done if the narrator had carried on playing on the chair?

_____

_____

3 Find each word in the text and write its meaning.

weird _____

queasy _____

How much did you do?   Questions 1–3

Circle a star to show how much you have done.

Some

Most

All

Fable: The Sun and the Wind

The Wind loved to boast about how strong he was. The Sun argued that it was just as important to be gentle.

'I like to show how strong I am,' declared the Wind. 'You sit in the sky and do nothing except shine. I am full of energy.'

'Hmmm…' said the Sun, looking thoughtful. 'I have an idea. Let's have a contest to see which of us is the most powerful.'

'I know who will win,' said the Wind.

'We shall see,' replied the Sun.

They looked down from the sky, watching the Earth below. A woman was walking along a pavement, wearing a bright yellow coat. 'Let's see which one of us is strong enough to take her coat off,' suggested the Sun.

'That woman down there?' puffed the Wind. 'I bet I can easily blow her coat off.'

'Okay,' said the Sun. 'Let's see you try.'

The Wind blew. The trees began to rustle their leaves. The woman looked up and frowned. The Wind blew harder. The trees began to move more quickly. The woman buttoned up her coat. The Wind blew as hard as he could. The trees began to sway wildly. Rubbish flew through the air. Washing blew off lines. The woman clutched her coat to her body as tightly as she could. 'Ooooff, I give up,' croaked the Wind. 'I have no huff or puff left.' He collapsed sulkily in a heap.

'My turn then,' smiled the Sun. She gently breathed and shone down onto the Earth. The air grew warmer. The woman looked up at the sky in surprise and laughed. The Sun breathed a little bit harder. The Earth grew warmer. The trees stretched up in delight and the woman unbuttoned her coat.

'Now watch,' whispered the Sun. She breathed one more time.

The woman took off her coat and mopped her brow. 'What strange weather there is today,' she thought to herself. 'I might just sit and enjoy this sun for five minutes.' She sat down on a bench and stretched out.

'How did you do that?' grumped the Wind. 'I used all my strength and I couldn't do it.'

'Easy,' replied the Sun. 'Gentle persuasion won the day. Sometimes rushing in and trying to force something to happen just doesn't work.'

Down on the Earth the woman nodded her head, as if she was agreeing with the Sun. 'That wind was strong, but the sun is stronger,' she murmured as she reached into her bag for her sunglasses.

A fable is a story, usually about animals or nature, which teaches a lesson.

1 Underline the correct answer.

What was the woman wearing?
a green coat   **a yellow coat**

What did the woman do when the Wind first began to blow?
she frowned   **she buttoned up her coat**

How did the Wind react when he failed?
he collapsed sulkily in a heap   **he shone down on the Earth**

What happened the second time the Sun breathed?
the woman looked up at the sky   **the trees stretched up in delight**

What did the woman reach for in her bag?
a hanky   **a pair of sunglasses**

2 Write all the words you can find that have been used instead of the word 'said'.

_____

_____

_____

Parent tip
Discuss the moral or lesson behind this type of story with your child.

3 What does 'mopped her brow' mean?

_____

Which phrases tell us how the woman felt when the sun began to shine?

_____

_____

What is the lesson, or the moral, of this story?

_____

_____

_____

How much did you do?   Questions 1–3

Circle a star
to show how much
you have done.

Some

Most

All

Non-fiction: Volcanoes fact file

- The word volcano comes from the name of the Roman god of fire, Vulcan.

- The Earth's crust is made up of huge slabs of rock, called tectonic plates. Volcanoes are most likely to occur at the points where two plates meet.

- Magma, which is a mixture of hot liquid rock and gas, can get squeezed up between the plates. When this happens, the magma needs somewhere to go!

- When the magma reaches the Earth's surface, it erupts as lava and ash.

- The lava cools and hardens to form new crust. After several eruptions, the rock builds up and a volcano forms.

- Volcanoes work a bit like a giant safety valve, allowing pressure to escape from inside the earth.

- Lava can reach temperatures of 1250°C. It burns and destroys everything in its path.

- There is an area of the Pacific Ocean known as the 'Pacific ring of fire', where over 75 per cent of the volcanoes on Earth are found.

- There are three different types of volcano:
  - **active** – a volcano that still erupts regularly
  - **dormant** – a volcano that has not erupted recently, but could still do so
  - **extinct** – a volcano that has not erupted for a long time and is very unlikely to do so.

- There are volcanoes under the sea.

- Mauna Loa is the world's largest active volcano. It is in Hawaii. It is 4169 metres high.

- Vesuvius is probably the world's most famous volcano. In 79 AD, it erupted, covering the Italian town of Pompeii in ash, destroying the town and killing its people. It is a popular tourist attraction today.

- There are around 1500 active volcanoes in the world today.

- More than 1 in 20 people live near to an active volcano.

- The soil around a volcano is very rich and fertile, which makes it perfect for growing crops.

A fact file is made up of lots of information about a specific topic.

1 Draw a line to the correct number to complete each fact.

Mauna Loa	79 AD
Number of people who live near a volcano	1250°C
Approximate number of active volcanoes in the world	1500
Lava temperature	4169 m
Eruption of Vesuvius	More than 1 in 20

2 Write a definition in your own words of the three types of volcano.

active _____

dormant _____

extinct _____

_____

3 Answer these questions using full sentences.

How is the information in this text organised?

_____

Why do you think it has been presented this way?

_____

4 What do you think it would be like to live near to an active volcano?
Why do people do it?
Explain your answer fully using evidence from the text.
Write your answer on a separate sheet of paper.

How much did you do? Questions 1–4

Circle a star to show how much you have done.

 Some

 Most

 All

Play script: The Skyfoogle

Narrator:	Once there was this man who turned up around our way and put up a tent in the local park. He placed posters all round the streets saying …
Man:	Come and see the most terrifying creature on earth – the Skyfoogle! At 2 o'clock tomorrow. A once in a lifetime opportunity!
Narrator:	Everyone was …
Reader 1:	Curious
Reader 2:	Mystified
Reader 3:	Excited.
Narrator:	So the next day, we all turned up to see …
All:	The fiercest animal in the entire world!
Narrator:	The man collected the money as we poured into the tent.
Man:	*(Man takes money as he speaks.)* Thank you sir. Thank you madam. Step right up! Step right up! Come and see the Skyfoogle! The most amazing creature the world has ever seen! Step right up!
Narrator:	There was a stage set up at one end of the tent, with a curtain in front of it.
Reader 1:	We all sat down and waited.
Reader 2:	The man went off behind the curtain.
Reader 3:	Suddenly we heard a terrible scream.
Man:	*(Voice offstage.)* Arrghhhh!
Narrator:	There was an awful yelling and crying and the noise of chains rattling.
FX:	*(A cacophony of noises offstage.)*
Narrator:	Suddenly the man came running onto the stage in front of the curtain. *(Man runs in.)* All his clothes were torn and there was blood on his face and he screamed at us …
Man:	Quick, get out, get out! Get out of here, THE SKYFOOGLE HAS ESCAPED!
All:	Arrghhhh!
Narrator:	We jumped up and ran out of the door and raced away as fast as we could. *(Everyone runs around scared and crosses to the other side of the stage. Man exits.)* But by the time we got ourselves together, the man had gone.
Reader 1:	We never saw him again.
Reader 2:	And we never saw our money again either.
Reader 3:	And none of us has ever seen …
All:	THE SKYFOOGLE!

A play based on a poem by Michael Rosen, adapted by Mark Carthew

A play is a story that can be acted out.

1 Answer these questions in full sentences.

What is the role of the narrator in the play?

_____

What are the stage directions (the words in brackets) for?

_____

What sort of setting do you imagine that the play takes place in?
Give **two** examples from the text for your answer.

_____

_____

2 What do the following words mean? Write a definition for each one.

curious _____

mystified _____

cacophony _____

3 Write answers for these questions using full sentences.
Give reasons for your answers.

How do you think the people in the audience felt when they saw the
man screaming and covered in blood?

_____

_____

How do you think they felt when they realised they had been tricked?

_____

_____

Parent tip
Read this play
aloud with your
child, using different
voices to develop
the different
characters.

How much did you do?   Questions 1–3

Circle a star
to show how much
you have done.

Some

Most

★
All

Modern poem: Write-A-Rap Rap

Hey, everybody, let's write a rap.
First there's a rhythm you'll need to clap.
Keep that rhythm and stay in time,
'cause a rap needs a rhythm and a good strong rhyme.

The rhyme keeps coming in the very same place
so don't fall behind and try not to race.
The rhythm keeps the rap on a regular beat
and the rhyme helps to wrap your rap up neat.

'But what'll we write?' I hear you shout.
There ain't no rules for what a rap's about.
You can rap about a robber, you can rap about a king,
you can rap about a chewed up piece of string...
(well, you can rap about almost... anything!)

You can rap about the ceiling, you can rap about the floor,
you can rap about the window, write a rap on the door.
You can rap about things that are mean or pleasant,
you can rap about wrapping up a Christmas present.

You can rap about a mystery hidden in a box,
you can rap about a pair of smelly old socks.
You can rap about something that's over and gone,
you can rap about something going on and on and on and on...

But when you think there just ain't nothing left to say...
you can wrap it all up and put it away.
It's a rap. It's a rap. It's a rap rap rap rap
RAP!

Tony Mitton

A rap poem matches rhymes to music or rhythm.

1 Number these sentences **1 to 6** to show the correct order in the poem.

There ain't no rules for what a rap's about.

and the rhyme helps to wrap your rap up neat.

so don't fall behind and try not to race.

The rhythm keeps the rap on a regular beat

'But what'll we write?' I hear you shout.

The rhyme keeps coming in the very same place

2 Read the poem aloud.

Find and write **two** examples of how the poet uses repetition of words to make a rhythm.

_____

_____

Find and write **four** examples of pairs of rhyming words.

_____

_____

Parent tip
Encourage your child to perform this poem out loud to get a sense of the rhythm and rhyme.

3 Write your own lines for this poem.

You can rap about _____, you can rap about _____.

You can rap about _____, you can rap about _____.

You can rap about _____, you can rap about _____.

You can rap about _____, you can rap about _____.

How much did you do?   Questions 1–3

Circle a star
to show how much
you have done.

 Some

 Most

 All

Character description: Bridget

Bridget. Our head teacher calls her Mrs Donnelly when she is praising her cooking in assembly, but everyone else calls her Bridget.

I don't know how old she is. Older than my mum, but younger than my granny. About 50, I think. She's not very tall. Some Year 6s are taller than her. Most of the time when I see her she is wearing a white overall and a pair of black lace-up shoes. She has to wear one of those hair net things, so it is quite hard to know what her hair is like, except I can see that it is dyed blonde. She has very bright blue eyes. Her cheeks are red. Or that might just be because she is hot all the time. All that steam and all that heat.

What I can see are her muscles. She has massive muscles in her arms. She can move really heavy trays of food all by herself. She also has massive calf muscles on her legs that bulge and twitch as she marches across the dinner hall. I told my dad about Bridget's leg muscles because they look like his cycling leg muscles. 'Lifting and shifting!' he said. Whatever that means.

When we go in to get our lunch, Bridget paces up and down behind the people who are serving the food. She watches what they are doing and never stops giving out instructions, unless it's to talk to one of us children. She is an amazing team captain. 'Too much pasta on that plate… give her a bigger baked potato… you need to go and get some more peas…' On and on and on. No wonder she can organise 576 meals a day!

She also sees what is going on. One day I went into the dining hall feeling all upset. Iris and Kayla weren't talking to me and Mr Griffiths had told me off for not doing my work in class. I couldn't because I was too busy thinking about the mean things that Iris had said. Bridget saw me sitting on my own. She came over to my table. She smiled at me and ruffled my hair. When she walked off I saw that she had left a folded napkin. I opened it and inside was one of her special biscuits. My favourite! I looked across at her. She smiled and winked.

Mind you, she can be fierce. When Zain and Callum started pushing and fighting with each other in the queue and frightening the younger children, Bridget came round the counter faster than Mo Farah and split them up. Go Bridget!

Last weekend we went to an Italian restaurant to celebrate my sister's birthday. Bridget was in there with some friends. She was wearing a sparkly red dress. Her hair was all soft and long and curly. I didn't recognise her at first until she smiled her big grin and said 'Hello Trouble.' Then she pointed to my pizza and whispered close to my ear, 'It's a bit heavy on the cheese don't you think? Not quite as good as mine!'

When I grow up I would like to be a wonder woman like Bridget.

A character has to have a personality, as well as a description of what they look like, to be believable.

1 Answer these questions about Bridget

Who is Bridget?
Tick (✓) the correct answer.

the head teacher ☐   the school cook ☐

a granny ☐   the narrator ☐

Parent tip
Talk to your child about who their favourite story characters are and why.

Find and copy **two** sentences that describe what Bridget looks like.

_____

_____

Circle the adjectives that best describe Bridget.

kind   slow   thoughtful   lazy   organised   decisive   funny

2 Look at the paragraph beginning: Last weekend…

Why doesn't the author recognise Bridget at first when they meet in the Italian restaurant?

_____

_____

3 Answer these questions.

Give **one** reason why you think the narrator was feeling upset in the dining hall.

_____

How do you think the author felt when Bridget gave her the biscuit?

_____

4 How do you think the author feels about Bridget?
Explain your answer fully, using evidence from the text.
Write your answer on a separate sheet of paper.

How much did you do?   Questions 1–4

Circle a star
to show how much
you have done.

Some

Most

All

News article: The escaping gorilla

London Zoo gorilla broke enclosure glass twice before escape

Although the zoo maintains Kumbuka did not break glass on Thursday, the 'destructive' silverback has form

A silverback gorilla that escaped from its enclosure at London Zoo has broken panes of glass at the attraction at least twice, the zoo has confirmed.

Visitors were locked in tea rooms and gift shops for an hour and armed police rushed to the zoo on Thursday evening after Kumbuka, a dominant male, broke out of his enclosure into a secure keepers' area before being tranquilised by vets and returned to his den.

ZSL (Zoological Society of London) London Zoo said it was carrying out a full investigation into the event but described it as a "minor incident", insisting that the 29-stone (184 kg) animal had "categorically" not broken any glass during the escape.

But the Guardian has learned that the gorilla, which the zoo has previously described as being "a little bit on the destructive side", has twice broken windows at the large enclosure, most recently this spring. In that incident, keepers were unable to say if he had thrown a missile or himself at the glass, but determined from a footprint on the glass that Kumbuka had been responsible for the damage.

A spokeswoman said on Friday night that windows in the Gorilla Kingdom were triple-laminated and that at no point had the gorilla smashed through the glass, which was designed to stay in its frame even if shattered. "ZSL London Zoo has recorded no events involving Kumbuka over the past six months that have raised concerns about safety," the zoo said in a statement.

Sources have claimed that the animal was able to get into the keepers' area, a double-height, caged-off section running along one side of the enclosure, after a door was left open. The zoo said it could not confirm any details about the cause until an investigation into the incident had concluded.

London Zoo says no member of the public was at risk, yet the incident inevitably has echoes of an incident at Cincinnati Zoo in May.

On Friday, the morning after the night before, all was calm in Gorilla Kingdom. In the indoor section of the animals' den, a very large room crammed with ropes, logs and hammocks, a female was chewing on a leafy branch while an infant swung from a knotted rope, provoking squeals of delight from a group of watching schoolchildren.

From www.theguardian.com by Esther Addley

A newspaper article informs readers about things that are happening in the world.

1 Underline the correct definition for each word.

destructive   breaks things so badly that they cannot be repaired

large and powerful

greedy

dominant   the biggest

the most powerful, in charge

the oldest

Parent tip
Discuss the meaning of any words or phrases in the article that your child has not come across before.

Parent tip
Encourage your child to find words and phrases that try to persuade you to think a certain way.

2 Find words or phrases in the article to answer these questions.

Find **three** phrases or sentences that suggest the gorilla may be dangerous.

_____

_____

_____

Find **three** phrases or sentences that the spokeswoman for the zoo uses to persuade the public that this is not true.

_____

_____

_____

3 Do you think that having the gorilla in the zoo is dangerous or not?
Give **two** reasons for your answer.

_____

_____

How much did you do?   Questions 1–3

Circle a star
to show how much
you have done.

Some   Most   All

25

Diary extract: A Roman soldier on Hadrian's Wall

Monday 4 March 129 AD

Today I have been here for half a year. I will never get used to this cold. Marcus Aurelius has been here for two years and he told me it will begin to get warmer soon. We saw some small flowers today when we were out patrolling the wall and he says that they are a sign that better times are coming. I hope so! If it's not cold, it's rain and cold together. How I wish I were home, in the sunshine. Cold and bored, bored and cold.

Tuesday 5 March 129 AD

I don't even mind having mud all over my legs any more. It helps to keep them a bit warmer. No sentry duty for me today. I was pleased. At least I would be inside the fort and not patrolling the wall, where some dirty, hairy Briton might fancy his chances with me. What could be worse? Er, cleaning latrines, that's what. 'The fort's getting bigger, we have more men, we have more latrines to clean,' said that really annoying officer with the big hooky nose (like the imperial eagle) and the annoying smirk. 'You do it then!' I thought, but I didn't say anything. Not worth it. So I wasn't cold today. Just worked like a slave at the Emperor's court instead. My hands are covered in blisters and cuts. My back is aching.

Wednesday 6 March 129 AD

Still cold. Still raining. Sentry duty today, so in the fort, but on my guard. Well, sort of. Was with Julius Romanus. He's a bit of a cheeky chap. Always got an idea or looking for a way to amuse himself. He had a pocketful of pebbles today and he'd made up a game, so he showed me how to play it. It was fun and we got so absorbed that we forgot what we should actually be doing. Suddenly I heard a noise and saw one of our officers heading our way. I stood up quickly and made out that I was staring out into the gloom. Julius wasn't as quick, so he got a kick up the backside and his stones scattered everywhere. No hard feelings though. He wasn't bothered. Tomorrow we've been put in the kitchens on a double shift as a punishment. Julius reckons we'll be able to pinch a load of food and sell it to the others.

Thursday 7 March 129 AD

Exhausted but not cold. Been standing near fires for most of the day, so for once I've been warm. It wasn't that bad. I was too scared to sneak any food out, but I managed to get quite a bit extra to eat. Julius was messing about too much and annoyed the head cook, so he was sent out into the yard to grind grains. In the cold and the wet. He didn't seem to mind. He was still clowning around.

Friday 8 March 129 AD

Marcus Aurelius got a letter from his parents today. It's only taken two years to get here. Still cold. Still wet. By the power of Jupiter, I want to go home.

Diary entries are written in the first person.

1 Answer these questions.

What time of year is it? _____

What word is used instead of 'toilets'? _____

How many different jobs did the soldier do this week? _____

What is the 'gloom'? _____

2 After reading this diary, would you like to have been a Roman soldier? Use the text to give **three** reasons for your answer.

_____

_____

_____

3 The narrator and Julius Romanus get in trouble with the officers and head cook. Find **two** examples from the text of how the men deal with the situations differently. An example has been given.

Julius Romanus	The narrator
He wasn't bothered.	Worked like a slave

Parent tip
Encourage your child to write their own diary during the holidays.

How much did you do?   Questions 1–3

Circle a star to show how much you have done.

Some   Most   All

27

Letter: Dear Mr Pig

21 Amley Avenue

Bristol

BS4 2DW

Dear Mr Pig,

I enjoyed meeting you and your charming family yesterday. Thank you for asking me to give you a quote to build three houses. I am putting together some initial costings, but please find below some further details that I think you might find useful when making your decision.

There are of course advantages and disadvantages with each type of building material.

Straw looks fabulous, especially on a sunny summer afternoon, but can be unreliable in windy weather conditions. It is currently £6 a bale with a 'buy one bale, get one free' offer running until 22 September at the local DIY store. This is the cheapest option. A straw house will cost £1,800.

Sticks are extremely eco-friendly, especially as we can obtain recycled branches sourced from Traditional Tale Wood, but open fires can be tricky in wooden buildings. Sticks are currently selling for £8 per bundle. I could build a stick house in the same style as the straw house for £4,200.

Bricks are certainly strong and long-lasting, but can be very expensive to build with. Bricks are £10 each, with a special offer of free cement with a purchase of 100 bricks or more. I could build you a brick house in the same style for £16,500.

I am sure you would like some time to discuss these options with your family, but please do let me know if you have any questions.

We can also provide extras such as:

- doors with security peepholes, so that you don't have to answer your door to strangers

- windbreaks in the garden to protect the house from strong winds

- anti-climbing paint to stop anyone from getting on the roof

- super-fast water heating systems.

I look forward to hearing from you soon.

Yours sincerely,

BB Wolf

Master Builder (Cunning Plan Building Company)

Letters can be written in different language styles.

1 Where do the sticks used to build the stick house come from? _____

Fill in the table to help Mr Pig decide which type of house to have built.

	advantages	disadvantages
straw		
sticks		
bricks		

How much more expensive is a stick house than a straw house? _____

Which house would you choose and why?

_____

_____

Parent tip
Ask your child to write a thank you letter, to practise using a formal style.

2 Which famous traditional tale is this letter based on? _____

'I enjoyed meeting you and your charming family yesterday.'
Which **two** phrases does BB Wolf use to please and flatter Mr Pig?

_____

Who might want to climb on the roof of a house? _____

Why would a super-fast water heating system be useful?

_____

Why do you think the building company is called 'Cunning Plan'?

_____

Why do you think BB Wolf is keen to build the houses for the three little pigs?

_____

How much did you do? Questions 1–2

Circle a star to show how much you have done.

Some

Most

All

Modern poem: Dear Mum

Dear Mum

While you were out
a cup went and broke itself,
a crack appeared in the blue vase
your great-great granddad
brought back from Mr Ming in China.
Somehow, without me even turning on the tap,
the sink mysteriously overflowed.
A strange jam-stain,
about the size of a boy's hand,
appeared on the kitchen wall.
I don't think we will ever discover
exactly how the cat
managed to turn on the washing-machine
(especially from the inside),
or how Sis's pet rabbit went and mistook
the waste-disposal unit for a burrow.
I can tell you I was scared when,
as if by magic,
a series of muddy footprints
appeared on the new white carpet.
I was being good
(honest)
but I think the house is haunted, so,
knowing you're going to have a fit,
I've gone over to Gran's for a bit.

Brian Patten

Dear Mum is modern poem with lots of funny images.

1 Make a list of **four** things that went wrong in the house while Mum was out.

_____

_____

_____

_____

2 Answer these questions with full sentences.

Who do you think the narrator of the poem is?

_____

How do you know the narrator is worried about what Mum will say?

_____

_____

What do you think Mum's reaction might be when she sees everything that has happened?

_____

Parent tip
Look out for poems about things within your child's experience as a good introduction to poetry.

3 How do you think the poet makes the poem funny? Give an example.

_____

_____

4 What do you think the poet is trying to do when he uses these words and phrases?

**broke itself   mysteriously overflowed
I don't think we will ever discover   as if by magic**

_____

How much did you do?   Questions 1–4

Circle a star
to show how much
you have done.

Some

Most

All

Classic fiction: Heidi

Uncle Alp had made a wooden seat and fixed it to the side of the hut looking over the valley. Here he was sitting peacefully, with his pipe in his mouth and his hands on his knees as the little party approached. Peter and Heidi ran ahead of Detie for the last part of the way, and Heidi was actually the first to reach the old man. She went straight up to him and held out her hand. 'Hallo, Grandfather,' she said.

'Hey, what's that?' he exclaimed gruffly, staring searchingly at her as he took her hand. She stared back, fascinated by the strange-looking old man, with his long beard and bushy grey eyebrows. Meanwhile, Detie came towards them, while Peter stood watching to see what would happen.

'Good morning, Uncle,' said Detie. 'I've brought you Tobias's daughter. I don't suppose you recognise her as you haven't seen her since she was a year old.'

'Why have you brought her here?' he demanded roughly. 'And you be off with your goats,' he added to Peter. 'You're late, and don't forget mine.' The old man gave him such a look that Peter disappeared at once.

'She's come to stay with you, Uncle,' Detie told him, coming straight to the point. 'I've done all I can for her these four years. Now it's your turn.'

'My turn, is it?' snapped the old man, glaring at her. 'And when she starts to cry and fret for you, as she's sure to do, what am I supposed to do then?'

'That's your affair,' retorted Detie. 'Nobody told me how to set about it when she was left on my hands, a baby barely a year old. Goodness knows I had enough to do, looking after Mother and myself. But now I've got to go away to a job. You're the child's nearest relative. If you can't have her here, do what you like with her. But you'll have to answer for it if she comes to any harm, and I shouldn't think you'd want anything more on your conscience.'

Detie was really far from easy in her mind about what she was doing, which was why she spoke so disagreeably, and she had already said more than she meant to.

The old man got up at her last words. She was quite frightened by the way he looked at her, and took a few steps backward.

'Go back where you came from and don't come here again in a hurry,' he said angrily, raising his arm.

From Heidi *by Johanna Spyri*

Heidi is a children's story that has been popular for many years.

1 Put a tick (✓) for true or a cross (✗) for false.

Peter looks after goats.

Detie is going on holiday.

Heidi is scared of Grandfather.

Grandfather is annoyed with Detie.

Detie likes Grandfather.

Parent tip
Classic fiction can be more challenging, because of its different language style.

2 Find and copy **four words or phrases** from the text that show Grandfather was annoyed and surprised when the visitors arrive.

_____

_____

3 Answer these questions with full sentences.

How do you think Grandfather is feeling about meeting Heidi?

_____

_____

Why do you think Detie is worried about leaving Heidi?

_____

_____

What do you think might happen if Heidi stays with Grandfather?

_____

_____

How much did you do?   Questions 1–3

Circle a star to show how much you have done.

Some

Most

All

Non-fiction: Rocks

The Earth has a hard outer layer of rock, which is called a crust.

The diagram below shows the different layers that make up the Earth.

1 The Earth's crust forms the outer layer.

2 The layer under the Earth's crust is called the mantle.

3 The centre of the Earth is called the core. There is an inner and an outer core. The outer core is liquid and is so hot that the rocks and metal in it have all melted. The liquid rock is called magma. This is what you see coming out of an erupting volcano as red-hot lava. The inner core is believed to be more like a solid ball of different metals.

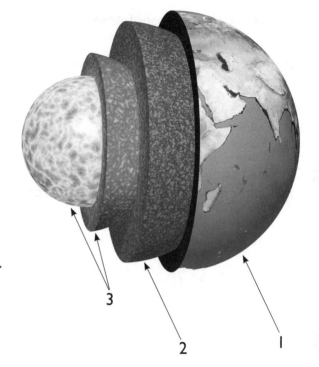

The crust is made up of three different types of rock:

- igneous rock

- sedimentary rock

- metamorphic rock.

The rocks are all made of minerals, but they were formed in different ways.

Look at the table below to find out how rocks are formed.

Igneous rocks	Sedimentary rocks	Metamorphic rocks
Melted rock, called magma, from the Earth's core, cools and hardens.	Rocks break down and are worn away by water. The sediment formed settles at the bottom of lakes and the sea, where it is compressed over millions of years to form new rocks.	Rocks far below the surface of the Earth are crushed by the weight of the crust and / or heated by the core to make a new type of very hard rock.

Diagrams are often used in non-fiction works to make explanations clearer.

1 Label the different layers of the Earth.

_____   _____

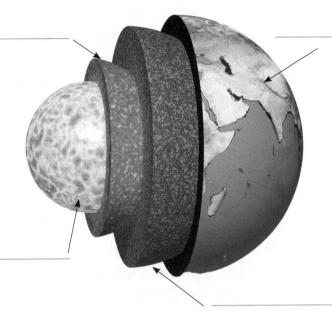

_____

_____

2 Circle the correct word.

Liquid rock is called **magnan** / **magnum** / **magma**.

When it cools, it forms **igneous** / **iguana** / **ignatius** rocks.

The crust is the **middle** / **inner** / **outer** layer.

Parent tip
Discuss with your child what different diagrams and drawings show.

3 Write a description in your own words for each type of rock.

metamorphic _____

_____

sedimentary _____

_____

igneous _____

_____

How much did you do?   Questions 1–3

Circle a star to show how much you have done.

Some   Most   All

35

Modern fiction: Flat Stanley

It was very dark in the main hall. A little bit of moonlight came through the windows, and Stanley could just make out the world's most expensive painting on the opposite wall. He felt as though the bearded man with the violin and the lady on the couch and the half-horse person and the winged children were all waiting, as he was, for something to happen.

Time passed and he got tireder and tireder. Anyone would be tired this late at night, especially if he had to stand in a picture frame balancing on little spikes.

Maybe they won't come, Stanley thought. Maybe the sneak thieves won't come at all.

The moon went behind a cloud and then the main hall was pitch dark. It seemed to get quieter, too, with the darkness. There was absolutely no sound at all. Stanley felt the hair on the back of his neck prickle beneath the golden curls of the wig.

Cr-eee-eee-k …

The creaking sound came from right out in the middle of the hall and even as he heard it Stanley saw, in the same place, a tiny yellow glow of light!

The creaking came again and the glow got bigger. A trap door had opened in the floor and two men came up through it into the hall!

Stanley understood everything all at once.

From Flat Stanley *by Jeff Brown*

Flat Stanley is a piece of fiction about a boy, Stanley, who was flattened when a notice board fell on him.

1 Answer these questions using full sentences.

The story mentions 'the bearded man with the violin and the lady on the couch and the half-horse person and the winged children'.
Who do you think they are?

_____

'Stanley understood everything all at once.'
What do you think Stanley had understood?

_____

Why does Stanley feel 'the hair on the back of his neck prickle'?

_____

_____

Where is Stanley hiding?

_____

2 How does the author make the mood feel scary?
Find **two** examples in the text.

_____

_____

3 Find **three words or phrases** that the author uses to describe the night-time.

_____

4 Circle the correct answer.

Who were the two men?	**night security staff**	**thieves**
What made the creaking sound?	**the glow of light**	**the trap door**
Where is this scene set?	**an art museum**	**a school hall**
Some light came from:	**the moon**	**the streetlight**

Parent tip
If your child enjoys a story, look for similar stories to encourage them to read more.

How much did you do?   Questions 1–4

Circle a star to show how much you have done.

Some

Most

All

Non-fiction: The Altamira cave paintings

In autumn 1879, a very exciting discovery was made in the region of Cantabria in Northern Spain. A Spanish nobleman and archaeologist called Marcelino Sanz de Sautuloa was exploring a cave in the hillside of Altamira, not far from his family's estate. He was very interested in finding out about the prehistoric past. His 8-year-old daughter, Maria, was with him.

At that time, most archaeologists believed that people from prehistoric times were 'savages', only a little more developed than apes and not really able to do anything.

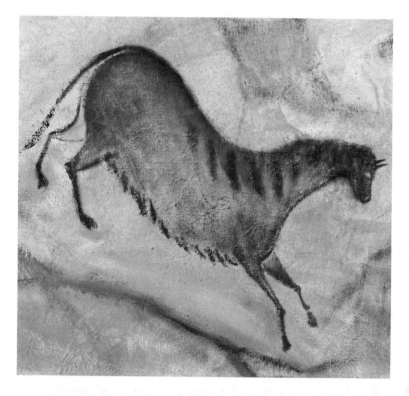

Sautuloa was digging in the floor of the cave, looking for prehistoric bones and tools when Maria shouted, 'Papi, I have found some oxen.' He went to find her, to see what she had found, and came upon a ceiling covered with dozens of paintings of aurochs, a type of ox that had been extinct for a long, long time.

'I was overcome with amazement. What I saw made me so excited I could hardly speak,' he later wrote. Maria had found the first gallery of prehistoric paintings ever to be discovered! They had been created between 18,500 and 14,000 years ago, by early human beings.

There were many archaeologists who could not believe they were real, because they were such good drawings and in excellent condition. Sautuloa was accused of forging them or having them produced by an artist.

At a prehistoric conference in Lisbon in 1880, specialists made fun of Sautuloa's findings and said that they could not be possible. It was not until 1902, following several other findings of prehistoric paintings, that archaeologists admitted that Sautuloa was right. Sadly, by that time Sautuloa had died, so he never lived to see the importance of his discovery acknowledged.

The importance of some historic events is not understood until much later in time.

1 Draw a line to match each word to its definition.

archaeologist	a member of a rich family
auroch	a person who looks at buried remains to discover how people lived in the past
forging	an ancient species of ox
nobleman	creating or imitating something and trying to pass it off as an original piece of work

2 Why do you think other archaeologists did not believe Sautuloa?

_____

_____

_____

3 Circle the correct answer.

What time of year was it when the paintings were discovered?

August   **autumn**

Sautuloa was:

an architect   **an archaeologist**

The paintings were discovered in:

Lisbon   **Spain**

Maria found:

paintings   **oxen**

> **Parent tip**
> Discuss what it would be like to live in a time without modern science and technology.

Legend: The Trojan horse

Over 3000 years ago, the Trojans and Greeks fought a long, terrible war. One of the reasons for the war was that Helen, the wife of the Greek king Menelaus, had been taken by Paris, son of the king of Troy.

The Greeks wanted to capture the Trojan city of Troy and take Helen back. They had been trying to do this for about 10 years. They could not get past the tall, strong city walls but at the same time, the Trojans did not seem able to drive the Greeks away. The Greeks began to think that if they could not win the battle with their physical strength, then they should win it with their brains.

Odysseus, a Greek general, had a clever idea. He ordered his workers to build a beautiful and huge wooden horse, large enough to hide men inside. The Trojans watched the giant horse being built and wondered what the Greeks were doing. Some thought that the Greeks were preparing a gift, as the symbol of Troy was a horse. Others hoped that it meant the war was going to end. It was all very mysterious.

Then one day, all the Greek army tents and armies began to disappear. The Trojans saw the Greek armies sailing away. After a few days, the only thing that remained was the tall strange, wooden horse. The people of Troy rushed outside, cheering. They thought that the Greeks had finally given up hope of capturing the city. They dragged the horse inside the city gates, which is just what Odysseus thought they would do. The king was proud of what he thought they had done in defeating the Greeks and wanted to show off the horse as a symbol of their victory.

The Trojans celebrated for hours before falling asleep. Then the Greeks played out the rest of their trick. Not all of the Greeks had sailed away on the warships. Odysseus had chosen some tough fighting men to hide inside the hollow wooden horse. These soldiers stepped out in the dark and opened the Trojan city gates. The Greek army, who had been in hiding, swarmed in.

The Greeks caught the Trojans completely off guard. After a fierce battle they captured the city and took Helen back to Greece.

A legend is an ancient story. It is usually a mixture of true and made-up events.

1 Find the missing words in the text to complete these sentences.

Almost 3000 years ago, the _____ and Greeks fought a long, terrible war.

Odysseus was a Greek _____.

The Trojans thought the _____ was a gift.

The Trojan King felt _____ when he thought he had defeated the Greeks.

There were _____ hidden inside the horse.

Parent tip
Stories like this can spark a child's interest and help to bring history to life.

2 Circle the correct answer.

How did the Trojans react when they saw the Greeks building the horse?

They liked it   **They were puzzled**   **They wanted to burn it**

Who had been captured by the Trojans?

Paris   **Menelaus**   **Helen**

The Trojans:

fell asleep.   **sailed away.**   **built the wooden horse.**

3 Answer the following questions using full sentences.

How do you think Odysseus felt when he realised his plan was going to work?

_____

_____

How do you think the Trojans felt when they realised they had been tricked?

_____

_____

How much did you do?   Questions 1–3

Circle a star to show how much you have done.

 Some

 Most

All

Story from another culture: The village of 'Couldn't be bothered'

Once upon a time there was a village where all the people were exceedingly lazy. They didn't keep their streets clean and they couldn't be bothered to weed their vegetable patches. The chief of the village hated it and every so often he would ask his people to clean up. Only a handful of people ever did and, even then, they would stop after one or two days. In the blink of an eye, the place would be just as bad again as it ever was.

One day a hurricane blew through the town. An enormous tree was blown over, right across the main road leading to the market place.

A trader came along, carrying his produce, and found the road blocked by the tree. He said, 'I haven't got time to move this tree! I've got to get my produce to the market!' So he walked around the tree and carried on his way. A second and a third trader came along and did exactly the same thing.

The chief heard about the tree blocking the road. He asked, 'Why don't some of these people get together and move it?' But days went by and nobody did anything about it.

The chief decided to teach his people a lesson. Very early the next day, before the sun had come up, he got some of his servants to dig a hole under the tree, where he hid some gold and then covered it up again. He made them swear to keep this a secret. Back at his palace, he instructed his town crier to gather all the citizens that afternoon at the tree.

When they were all together, the chief made a speech to his people suggesting that if all of them worked together, it would not take very long to remove the obstacle. One of the farmers said, 'The hurricane put that tree there. Let's ask the hurricane to move it out of the way.'
'Yes,' said another. 'Why should we exert ourselves?'
'What's wrong with walking around it?' asked another.

The chief was exasperated. He was just about to give up when a skinny young man stepped forward. He was a poor farmer. 'I will have a go,' he said, and started pulling and pushing to shift the heavy tree.

The chief waited for a short while to see if anybody would come forward to help the young man. When nobody did, he instructed his servants to lend a hand. Once the tree had been moved to the side of the road, the Chief went up to the young farmer and took him to the spot where he'd buried the gold that morning. The chief told him to dig there, and promised him that he could keep whatever he found there. The young farmer started digging and very quickly uncovered the gold. He was overjoyed.

The chief said to him, 'All this gold is yours to keep. You deserve it and you can do with it as you please.' To the lazy village people he said, 'Let this be a lesson to you all! Rewards come to the person who is prepared to work hard.'

This is a story from another culture with a moral to teach.

1 Use a dictionary to find definitions of these words.

exceedingly _____

exasperated _____

overjoyed _____

exert _____

2 What did the chief find so annoying about the village people?

_____

Give **two** examples of things that the people would not do to keep the village tidy.

_____

_____

Find and write **two** excuses that people made for not moving the tree.

_____

_____

What lesson was the chief trying to teach the village people?

_____

_____

3 **Who said this? Write the name of the character.**

'I've got to get my produce to the market!' _____

'I will have a go.' _____

How much did you do? Questions 1–3

Circle a star to show how much you have done.

 Some

 Most

 All

Classic poem: What is pink?

What is pink? A rose is pink
By the fountain's brink.

What is red? A poppy's red
In its barley bed.

What is blue? The sky is blue
Where the clouds float through.

What is white? A swan is white
Sailing in the light.

What is yellow? Pears are yellow,
Rich and ripe and mellow.

What is green? The grass is green,
With small flowers between.

What is violet? Clouds are violet
In the summer twilight.

What is orange? Why, an orange,
Just an orange!

Christina Rossetti

Christina Rossetti was a Victorian poet. She lived from 1830 to 1894.

1 Write the pairs of rhyming words from the poem.
The first pair has been done for you.

pink + brink

_____   _____

_____   _____

_____   _____

Parent tip
This is a good introduction to classic poetry as the language and meaning are quite accessible.

2 The poet has used **repetition** throughout the poem.
What does this mean? Find an example.

_____

_____

3 Fill in the missing words.

What is yellow? _____ are yellow,
Rich and ripe and mellow.

What is white? A swan is _____
Sailing in the light.

_____ is green? The grass is green

With _____ flowers in between.

4 Write two lines about each of these colours that could be added to the poem.

What is black? _____

_____

What is brown? _____

_____

How much did you do?   Questions 1–4

Circle a star
to show how much
you have done.

Some

Most

All

Historical fiction: Boudicca

Boudicca was queen of the Iceni people of eastern England. She is often called 'the Warrior Queen', as she led a major uprising against the Romans.

A Roman writer of the time described Boudicca as 'possessed of greater intelligence as often belongs to women'. She was said to be tall, with long reddish brown hair, a harsh voice and a piercing glare. Her name means 'victory'. She wore a large golden necklace, a colourful tunic and a thick cloak fastened by a brooch.

Boudicca was married to Prasutagus and they had two daughters. When the Romans conquered Southern England in 43 AD, they allowed Prasutagus to continue to rule as King. However, when Prasutagus died, the Romans decided to rule the Iceni directly and took away lots of their land and property. They are also said to have attacked Boudicca and her daughters. This all made the Iceni very angry.

Around 60 AD, the Roman governor Paulinus was busy fighting in North Wales. The Iceni tribe, led by Boudicca, rebelled. Members of other tribes joined them. Boudicca and her army attacked and destroyed Colchester, which was then the capital of Roman Britain. The Romans sent the Ninth Legion of 4000 men to stop Boudicca and her rebels, but they were ambushed and defeated. The rebels then attacked London and St Albans, burning the Roman cities to the ground and killing their inhabitants. They are said to have killed up to 80,000 people!

Boudicca and her army were finally defeated by Paulinus in 61 AD. Paulinus chose the site of the final battle carefully to suit his army. Even though there were far fewer Romans, they had better weapons and training, which enabled them to totally defeat the Britons. No one knows exactly where the final battle between Boudicca and the Roman forces took place. However, it is believed to have taken place somewhere in the Midlands, near to Watling Street, an important road built by the Romans.

Boudicca is thought to have poisoned herself to avoid being captured.

Historical fiction blends fact and fictional details.

1 Describe what Boudicca looked like.

_____

_____

_____

2 Find the numbers to answer these questions.

What year did the Romans conquer Southern England? _____

How many people are Boudicca's army thought to have killed? _____

Which legion did Boudicca defeat at Colchester? _____

3 Which **three** towns and cities did Boudicca attack?

Parent tip
Find another version of Boudicca's story and talk to your child about how the details vary.

_____

Give **two** reasons why the Iceni were angry with the Romans.

_____

_____

4 Answer the questions with full sentences.

Why do you think the Romans were able to finally defeat Boudicca and her army?

_____

_____

Why do you think Boudicca did not want to be captured?

_____

_____

How much did you do?   Questions 1–4

Circle a star to show how much you have done.

Some

Most

All

Non-fiction: The life-cycle of a butterfly

The amazing change from a caterpillar to a butterfly is called a metamorphosis.

There are four clear stages.

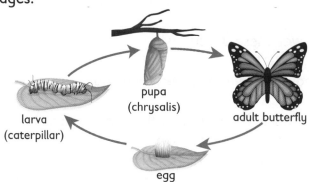

The first stage

A caterpillar egg is tiny. It is usually an oval or cylindrical shape.

The female caterpillar attaches its eggs to the leaves or stem of a plant, near to the food that the hatched caterpillar will need to eat.

The egg hatches out into a caterpillar.

The second stage

The caterpillar (or larva) is a long worm-like shape. Caterpillars have different colours or patterns depending on the type of butterfly they are going to be. Some caterpillars are covered in long hairs that cause an itchy skin reaction if touched.

Caterpillars eat and grow very quickly at this stage. They can shed their skin several times to cope with their growing body. Some caterpillars grow to be 100 times bigger than when they first hatch out of their egg!

The third stage

This is the the stage where the caterpillar transforms or changes. The fully grown caterpillar produces a pupa or chrysalis. A hard case forms around the pupa to protect it from the weather and predators. Inside the pupa, the caterpillar's body structure breaks down and the parts of an adult butterfly develop.

The fourth stage

When the butterfly is ready to emerge, the case around the pupa splits open. The butterfly cannot fly immediately, because its wings are too wet and wrinkled. Once the butterfly's wings have dried, the butterfly pumps a liquid into them called haemolymph. This makes the wings strong.

The cycle has ended. The butterfly flies off to search for food and a mate. Then the cycle will begin again.

A life-cycle describes the stages in a life from birth to death.

1 Write the number of the stage in which the event happens.

The butterfly produces a liquid called haemolymph.   ☐

The pupa has a hard case around it.   ☐

Caterpillars grow very quickly.   ☐

A butterfly attaches its eggs to a leaf or stem.   ☐

2 Write **one** fact about each of the following.

a caterpillar _____

a pupa _____

a butterfly _____

an egg _____

3 Is the life-cycle diagram easier to understand than the text?
Give a reason for your answer.

_____

_____

Why do you think the text has been organised into four stages?

_____

_____

_____

Parent tip
Your child needs to be able to interpret and understand diagrams as well as text.

How much did you do?   Questions 1–3

Circle a star
to show how much
you have done.

 Some

 Most

 All

Modern fiction: The Iron Man

The Iron Man came to the top of the cliff.

How far had he walked? Nobody knows. Where had he come from? Nobody knows. How was he made? Nobody knows.

Taller than a house, the Iron Man stood at the top of the cliff, on the very brink, in the darkness.

The wind sang through his iron fingers. His great iron head, shaped like a dustbin but as big as a bedroom, slowly turned to the right, slowly turned to the left. His iron ears turned, this way, that way. He was hearing the sea. His eyes, like headlamps, glowed white, then red, then infra-red, searching the sea. Never before had the Iron Man seen the sea.

He swayed in the strong wind that pressed against his back. He swayed forward, on the brink of the high cliff.

And his right foot, his enormous iron right foot, lifted—up, out, into space, and the Iron Man stepped forward, off the cliff, into nothingness.

CRRRAAAASSSSSSH!

Down the cliff the Iron Man came toppling, head over heels.

CRASH!

CRASH!

CRASH!

From rock to rock, snag to snag, tumbling slowly. And as he crashed and crashed and crashed

His iron legs fell off.

His iron arms broke off, and the hands broke off the arms.

His great iron ears fell off and his eyes fell out.

His great iron head fell off.

All the separate pieces tumbled, scattered, crashing, bumping, clanging, down on to the rocky beach far below.

A few rocks tumbled with him.

Then

Silence.

Only the sound of the sea, chewing away at the edge of the rocky beach, where the bits and pieces of the Iron Man lay scattered far and wide, silent and unmoving.

Only one of the iron hands, lying beside an old, sand-logged washed-up seaman's boot, waved its fingers for a minute, like a crab on its back. Then it lay still.

While the stars went on wheeling through the sky and the wind went on tugging at the grass on the cliff-top and the sea went on boiling and booming.

Nobody knew the Iron Man had fallen.

From The Iron Man *by Ted Hughes*

The Iron Man is a story that mixes fantasy with poetry.

1 Look at the following sections of text.

'How far had he walked? Nobody knows. Where had he come from? Nobody knows. How was he made? Nobody knows.'

The author has written in short, repetitive sentences.
Why do you think he has written in this way?

_____

_____

'CRRRAAAASSSSSSH!
Down the cliff the Iron Man came toppling, head over heels.
CRASH!
CRASH!
CRASH!'

Parent tip
Point out how the author uses repetition and poetic language to set the scene.

Why has the author chosen to place the words like this?

_____

_____

2 The author paints a very clear word picture of the Iron Man.
Find **two** things that he compares the Iron Man to.

_____

3 Do you think the Iron Man will survive his fall from the cliff? Explain your answer.

_____

_____

If he survives, what might happen to him next?

_____

How much did you do?　　Questions 1–3

Circle a star
to show how much
you have done.

Some

Most

All

Classic fiction: The Secret Garden

A boy was sitting under a tree, with his back against it, playing on a rough wooden pipe. He was a funny-looking boy about twelve. He looked very clean and his nose turned up and his cheeks were as red as poppies, and never had Mistress Mary seen such round and such blue eyes in any boy's face. And on the trunk of the tree he leaned against, a brown squirrel was clinging and watching him, and from behind a bush nearby a cock pheasant was delicately stretching his neck to peep out, and quite near him were two rabbits sitting up and sniffing with tremulous noses – and actually it appeared as if they were all drawing near to watch him and listen to the strange, low little call his pipe seemed to make.

When he saw Mary he held up his hand and spoke to her in a voice almost as low as and rather like his piping.

'Don't tha' move,' he said. 'It'd flight 'em.'

Mary remained motionless. He stopped playing his pipe and began to rise from the ground. He moved so slowly that it scarcely seemed as though he were moving at all, but at last he stood on his feet and then the squirrel scampered back up into the branches of his tree, the pheasant withdrew his head, and the rabbits dropped on all fours and began to hop away, though not at all as if they were frightened.

'I'm Dickon,' the boy said. 'I know tha'rt Miss Mary.'

Then Mary realised that somehow she had known at first that he was Dickon. Who else could have been charming rabbits and pheasants as the natives charm snakes in India? He had a wide, red, curving mouth and his smile spread all over his face.

'I got up slow,' he explained, 'because if tha' makes a quick move it startles 'em. A body 'as to move gentle an' speak low when wild things is about.'

He did not speak to her as if they had never seen each other before, but as if he knew her quite well. Mary knew nothing about boys, and she spoke to him a little stiffly because she felt rather shy. 'Did you get Martha's letter?' she asked.

He nodded his curly, rust-coloured head. 'That's why I come.'

He stooped to pick up something which had been lying on the ground beside him when he piped.

'I've got th' garden tools. There's a little spade an' rake an' a fork an' hoe. Eh! they are good 'uns. There's a trowel, too. An' th' woman in th' shop threw in a packet o' white poppy an' one o' blue larkspur when I bought th' other seeds.'

'Will you show the seeds to me?' Mary said.

She wished she could talk as he did. His speech was so quick and easy. It sounded as if he liked her and was not the least afraid she would not like him, though he was only a common moor boy, in patched clothes and with a funny face and a rough, rusty-red head. As she came closer to him she noticed that there was a clean fresh scent of heather and grass and leaves about him, almost as if he were made of them. She liked it very much and when she looked into his funny face with the red cheeks and round blue eyes she forgot that she had felt shy.

From The Secret Garden *by Frances Hodgson-Burnett*

The Secret Garden is a classic Victorian novel.

1 Answer these questions using full sentences.

Which animals are in the forest with Dickon?

_____

What is Dickon playing?

_____

How do you know Mary has not met Dickon before?

_____

What has Dickon brought for Mary?

_____

2 Who is it? Write **Mary** or **Dickon**.

_____ has curly red hair.

_____ does not know any boys.

_____ knows a lot about animals.

_____ wants to do some gardening.

3 Mary looks at Dickon very carefully.
Use these phrases to write **three** sentences that describe Dickon.

a common moor boy **patched clothes** **rough, rusty red hair** **funny face**
cheeks red as poppies **round blue eyes** **wide, red curving mouth**

_____

_____

_____

_____

How much did you do?   Questions 1–3

Circle a star
to show how much
you have done.

Some

Most

All

Answers

For questions that require full sentences, answers will vary. Example answers are given here. A correct answer will cover the same key points. An answer that covers an alternative valid point is acceptable, as long as it makes reference to / is supported by evidence from the text.

Page 5 – Modern fiction: The Worst Witch

1   Maud says, "I think I can remember it vaguely" and "Bits of it, anyway".

Any three adverbs / phrases that express doubt or uncertainty, e.g. vaguely; doubtfully; "Are you sure?"; not very definitely; "Absolutely sure?"

Child's own answer. Must include a reason related to the text, e.g.

Yes, I would let them make me a potion, because I think it would be funny if it went wrong.

No, I wouldn't let them make me a potion, because they don't seem to know what they are doing.

2   Mildred; vaguely; insisted

3   Mildred; Maud; Maud; Mildred

Page 7 – Persuasive writing: Acro"bats"

1   green; a helmet; Sawley; 70

2   **Any two from:** delicious; home-made; award-winning; organic

Any three verbs (words that describe an action) from: fly; hang; swing; leap; cross

red, orange, green

3   **Child's own answers, e.g.**

It makes you think of bats and acrobats. Bats are good at flying and acrobats are good at balancing.

It is telling you that the park is easy to get to.

The leaflet says that safety is a priority. The park provides helmets, gloves and safety harnesses and there is a safety talk before starting. It also mentions that there are trained guides.

Page 9 – Non-fiction: Contents page

1   transport; Ali Carson; 18; glossary

2   **Child's own answer.** Must contain a reference to transport.

It is organised into topics. / There is a contents page. / There is a glossary and index.

The index is at the back. / The index is on page 38.

You would look in the glossary.

3   10; 6; 22

Page 11 – Modern Poem: The sound collector

1   ticking – clock; popping – toaster; drumming – raindrops; swishing – curtain; gurgle – drain

2   **Child's own answer.** A choice of four sound verbs from the poem, e.g. hissing, squeaking, creaking, whistling, etc., with a reason for each answer.

3   **Child's own answer.** Should include ideas of sadness and loss / the idea of losing something / silence and things never being the same again (perhaps mentioning a stranger in black and grey).

4 **Child's own answer.** Must include references from the poem that back up their ideas.

Page 13 – Recount: A day at Mum's work

1 Friday; architect; hot chocolate; train; swivel chair

2 The train was very hot and sweaty because there were so many people on it.

Child's own answer, e.g. No, because they say, 'I'm glad I don't have to do that every day!'

The lady in the office might have asked the narrator to stop / spoken to their mum about it.

3 weird – strange / unusual; queasy – feels sick

Page 15 – Fable: The Sun and the Wind

1 a yellow coat; she frowned; he collapsed sulkily in a heap; the trees stretched up in delight; a pair of sunglasses

2 declared; replied; suggested; puffed; murmured; croaked; grumped; smiled; whispered; argued; replied

3 She wiped her face because she was hot.

The woman looked up at the sky in surprise and laughed / enjoyed the sun / stretched out.

You don't always get your own way by being powerful and pushy. Sometimes it is better to be gentle and persuade people round to your point of view.

Page 17 – Non-fiction: Volcanoes fact file

1 Mauna Loa – 4169 m

Number of people who live near a volcano – More than 1 in 20

Approximate number of active volcanoes in the world – 1500

Lava temperature – 1250°C

Eruption of Vesuvius – 79 AD

2 A volcano that still erupts regularly.

A volcano that erupts occasionally but is usually quiet.

A volcano that has not erupted for a long time and is not expected to do so again.

3 The information is organised in bullet points.

Child's own answer, e.g.

It is organised like this to make it easy to read / to focus just on the facts.

4 **Child's own answer.** Must refer to facts from the text, e.g.

I think it would be scary to live close to an active volcano in case it erupted, but people do it because   the land is good for growing crops.

Page 19 – Play script: The Skyfoogle

1 The narrator helps to tell the story. / The narrator explains what is happening.

The stage directions give instructions for sound effects / tell the actors where to stand / what to do.

Child's own answer, e.g.

I think the setting is like a circus because it is in a tent and the man says, 'Step right up! Step right up!' like a ringmaster.

2 curious – keen to know or learn something; mystified – very puzzled; cacophony – a mixture of sounds that don't sound good together

3 **Child's own answers.** Must refer to the text, e.g.

I think the people in the audience felt shocked and scared when they saw the man screaming and covered in blood.

I think they felt angry and wanted their money back when they realised they had been tricked.

Page 21 – Modern poem: Write-A-Rap Rap

1 6; 4; 2; 3; 5; 1

2 **Answers should quote directly from the text, e.g.**

You can rap about a robber, you can rap about a king, you can rap about a chewed up piece of string...; You can rap about a mystery hidden in a box, you can rap about a pair of old smelly socks.

Any four from: rap and clap; time and rhyme; place and race; beat and neat; shout and about; king and / or string and / or anything; floor and door; pleasant and present; box and socks; gone and on; say and away

3 **Answer should follow the rhythm of the text and use a pair of rhyming words, e.g.**

You can rap about a kitten, you can rap about a dog.
You can rap about a hamster, you can rap about a frog.
You can rap about a rabbit, you can rap about a hare.
You can rap about a tiger, you can rap about a bear.

Page 23 – Character description: Bridget

1 the school cook

Any two from: She's not very tall. / She has to wear one of those hair net things, so it is quite hard to know what her hair is like, except I can see that it is dyed blonde. / She has very bright blue eyes. / Her cheeks are red. / She has massive muscles in her arms. / She also has massive calf muscles on her legs that bulge and twitch as she marches across the dinner hall.

kind; thoughtful; organised; decisive; funny

2 **Child's own answer, e.g.**

She looks so different. She is all dressed up and has had her hair done. She is not in her work clothes.

3 Kayla and Iris had been mean to her. / Mr Griffiths had told her off.

Child's own answer, e.g.

I think the narrator felt happier / less miserable / cheered up.

4 **Child's own answer, e.g.**

I think the narrator likes Bridget because she says, 'When I grow up I would like to be a wonder woman like Bridget.' / because she gave her a biscuit / she thinks Bridget is good at her job.

Page 25 – News article: The escaping gorilla

1 destructive – breaks things so badly that they cannot be repaired; dominant – the most powerful, in charge

2 **Phrases that suggest the gorilla may be dangerous – any three from:** has broken panes of glass at the attraction at least twice;

broke out of his enclosure... before being tranquilised; a little bit on the destructive side; twice broken windows

Phrases that the spokeswoman for the zoo uses to assure the public that this is not true – any three from: minor incident; categorically not broken any glass; no events involving Kumbuka... have raised concerns about safety; no member of the public was at risk

3   **Child's own answer.** Answers must reference the text and include two different reasons for the opinion.

Page 27 – Diary extract: A Roman soldier on Hadrian's Wall

1   March / spring / end of winter

latrines

four

darkness / miserable weather

2   **Child's own answer.** Answers must reference the text, e.g.

I wouldn't have liked to be a soldier because I wouldn't like the cold / the horrible jobs / being away from home.

I would have liked to be a soldier because I would learn new things / get to travel / make new friends.

3

Julius Romanus	The narrator
Didn't seem to mind.	Didn't say anything.
Still clowning about.	Was scared to sneak food out.
Messing about and annoyed the cook.	Stood up quickly and made out he was staring into the gloom.

Page 29 – Letter: Dear Mr Pig

1   Traditional Tale Wood

	advantages	disadvantages
straw	cheap, looks fabulous	blows away in wind
sticks	cheap, recycled, from a local wood	burns easily
bricks	strong, long-lasting	expensive

£2400

Child's own answer. Must include a valid reason related to the text.

2   The three little pigs

'enjoyed meeting you'; 'charming family'

BB Wolf

To heat water for a cooking pot (accept: to heat water / the house)

Because BB Wolf is thinking of clever / crafty / sly ways to do bad things

So that he can build the houses badly and catch the pigs

Page 31 – Modern poem: Dear Mum

1   **Any four from:** a cup broke itself; the sink overflowed; a stain appeared on the kitchen wall; the cat turned the washing machine on; the rabbit went in the waste disposal; muddy footprints on the carpet; a valuable vase was cracked

2   The narrator of the poem is a child.

The narrator is worried about what mum will say because they try to make lots of excuses. They then say they have 'gone over to Gran's', so they won't be there when Mum arrives home.

Child's own answer, e.g. Mum will be very angry at all the damage.

3 The poet makes the poem funny by telling us lots of things that have gone wrong, for example, the cat in the washing machine.

4 Make us laugh by making excuses for the child / Make it sound ridiculous and unlikely, like something a child might make up.

Page 33 – Classic fiction: Heidi

1 ✓; ✗; ✗; ✓; ✗

2 **Any four words or phrases from the text that show that Grandfather was annoyed / surprised / shocked, e.g.** glaring at her; exclaimed gruffly; snapped; demanded roughly; he said angrily; raising his arm

3 **Child's own answer.** Must express an opinion, with reference to the text, e.g.

I think Grandfather is feeling surprised and shocked when he meets Heidi because he isn't expecting her / hasn't had time to get used to the idea / is worried that Heidi will miss Detie

Child's own answer. Must express an opinion, with reference to the text, e.g.

I think Detie is worried about leaving Heidi because Heidi and Grandfather don't know each other / they might not like each other / Detie doesn't like Grandfather.

Child's own answer. Must express an opinion, with reference to the text, e.g.

If Heidi stays with Grandfather, they might really like each other / Grandfather might have to find someone else to look after Heidi.

Page 35 – Non-fiction: Rocks

1

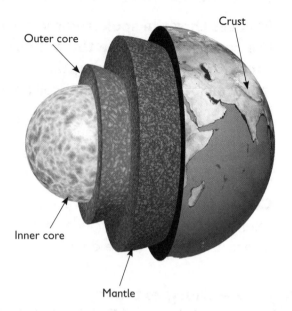

2 magma; igneous; outer

3 **Child's own answer.** Answers should reflect the descriptions given in the table on page 34, but must be written in the child's own words, e.g.

Metamorphic rocks are made when rocks below the Earth's surface are heated and / or put under pressure.

Sedimentary rocks are formed from sediment, made when old rocks are worn away, that is compressed over millions of years.

Igneous rocks are made when magma cools and hardens.

Page 37 – Modern fiction: Flat Stanley

1 They are characters in a painting.

Stanley had understood how the thieves had got into the building.

Stanley feels the hair on the back of his neck prickle because he feels scared / excited that something is going to happen.

He is in a picture frame.

2 **Any two from (with examples of some of the specific words used in the text):** He describes the dark; he describes the silence; he describes how Stanley is feeling; he describes the men coming.

3 **Any three from:** very dark; moonlight; pitch dark; late at night; glow; the moon went behind a cloud; no sound at all

4 thieves; the trap door; an art museum; the moon

Page 39 – Non-fiction: The Altamira cave paintings

1 archaeologist – a person who looks at buried remains to discover how people lived in the past

auroch – an ancient species of ox

forging – creating or imitating something and trying to pass it off as an original piece of work

nobleman – a member of a rich family

2 **Child's own answer, e.g.**
They didn't think it was possible that prehistoric people could draw / that the paintings would have lasted so long.

3 autumn; an archaeologist; Spain; paintings

Page 41 – Legend: The Trojan horse

1 Trojans; general; horse; proud; soldiers

2 They were puzzled; Helen; fell asleep.

3 **Child's own answer, e.g.**
I think he would have been really pleased / excited.

Child's own answer, e.g.
I think they would have been furious / scared / angry.

Page 43 – Story from another culture: The village of 'Couldn't be bothered'

1 exceedingly – extremely, very; exasperated – annoyed, frustrated; overjoyed – very happy, delighted; exert – to make yourself work, make an effort

2 They were so lazy.

clean the streets; weed their vegetable patches.

Any two from: no time; had to get stuff to market; the hurricane should move it; they could walk around it

That being so lazy wasn't a good thing and, if they worked hard, they would get a reward.

3 the first trader; the skinny man / poor farmer

Page 45 – Classic poem: What is pink?

1 red + bed; blue + through; white + light; yellow + mellow; green + between; violet + twilight

2 It means that she uses the same words, 'What is... ?', over and over again.

3 Pears; white; What; small

4 **Child's own answer.** Must follow the style and format of the poem, e.g.

What is black? A crow is black,
Sooty, like an old coal sack.
What is brown? A conker is brown,
Inside its green and spikey gown.

Page 47 – Historical fiction: Boudicca

1 **Child's own answer, e.g.**
She was clever, tall, with long reddish brown hair and a piercing glare. She wore a large golden necklace, a colourful tunic and a thick cloak fastened by a brooch.

2 43 AD; 80 000; Ninth

3 Colchester; London; St Albans

They had hurt Boudicca; they were taking away land

4 **Child's own answer, e.g.**
The Romans finally defeated Boudicca and her army because they had better weapons and were better trained.

Child's own answer, e.g.
I think Boudicca did not want to be captured because she knew that the Romans would be very cruel to her.

Page 49 – Non-fiction: The life-cycle of a butterfly

1 4; 3; 2; 1

2 **Accept any answers taken directly from the text, e.g.**

A caterpillar eats a lot and grows very quickly.

A pupa protects the caterpillar when it is changing into a butterfly.

A butterfly has wet and wrinkly wings when it first hatches.

A butterfly egg is shaped like a cylinder

3 **Child's own answer, e.g.**
Yes, because I find it easier to look at pictures, rather than read a lot of writing.

No, I prefer to read, rather than look at diagrams.

Child's own answer, e.g.
I think the text has been organised into four stages because the diagram of the life-cycle shows four stages / so that you can learn about each stage separately / because it makes it easier to understand.

Page 51 – Modern fiction: The Iron Man

1 **Child's own answer, e.g.**
I think he has done this to make the reader really think about the Iron Man. / I think he has done this to make the Iron Man seem mysterious / scary.

Child's own answer, e.g.
I think the author has chosen to place the words like this to make it look like the Iron Man is falling down.

2 **Any two from:** dustbin; house; bedroom; headlamps (his eyes)

3 **Child's own answer.** Must give a reason, e.g.

I think he will survive, because I think this is the beginning of the book and otherwise there won't be a story.

I think he won't survive because this sounds like the end of the story.

Child's own answer, e.g.
He might become a superhero and save the planet! / He is captured and chained up by people who are afraid of him.

**Page 53 – Classic fiction:
The Secret Garden**

1   Mary sees a squirrel, a cock pheasant and some rabbits.

    Dickon is playing a pipe.

    Mary hasn't met Dickon before because the text says 'never had Mistress Mary seen such round and such blue eyes' / the text says 'Mary knew nothing about boys' / Dicken introduces himself to her.

    He has brought her gardening tools and seeds.

2   Dickon; Mary; Dickon; Mary

3   **Child's own answer, e.g.**

    Dickon has rough, rusty red hair and a funny face.

    He has cheeks red as poppies, round blue eyes and a wide, red curving mouth.

    Mary says he is a common moor boy with patched clothes.

My words

Check your progress

- Shade in the stars on the progress certificate to show how much you did. Shade one star for every ⭐ you circled in this book.

- If you have shaded fewer than 20 stars, go back to the pages where you circled Some ☆ or Most ⭐ and try those pages again.

- If you have shaded 20 or more stars, well done!

- - - - - ✂ -

Collins Easy Learning Comprehension
bumper book Ages 7–9

Progress certificate
for

Name _____   Date _____

pages 4–5	pages 6–7	pages 8–9	pages 10–11	pages 12–13	pages 14–15	pages 16–17	pages 18–19	pages 20–21
⭐ 1	⭐ 2	⭐ 3	⭐ 4	⭐ 5	⭐ 6	⭐ 7	⭐ 8	⭐ 9

pages 22–23	pages 24–25	pages 26–27	pages 28–29	pages 30–31	pages 32–33	pages 34–35	pages 36–37	pages 38–39
⭐ 10	⭐ 11	⭐ 12	⭐ 13	⭐ 14	⭐ 15	⭐ 16	⭐ 17	⭐ 18

pages 40–41	pages 42–43	pages 44–45	pages 46–47	pages 48–49	pages 50–51	pages 52–53
⭐ 19	⭐ 20	⭐ 21	⭐ 22	⭐ 23	⭐ 24	⭐ 25

Did you find and colour all 27 bookworms?

(Including this one!)